What is a Still Life?

Ruth Thomson

W
FRANKLIN WATTS
LONDON•SYDNEY

First published in 2004 by Franklin Watts
338 Euston Road, London NW1 3BH

Franklin Watts Australia, Hachette Children's Books
Level 17/207 Kent Street, Sydney NSW 2000

Editor: Caryn Jenner
Design: Sphere Design
Art director: Jonathan Hair
Picture Research: Diana Morris

The publisher wishes to thank Fiona Cole for her assistance with the artwork and activities in this book.
Thanks also to Peggy Leonard, Edward Holmes, Sophie Peutrill, Imani Jawarah and Aprile Field.

All photographs taken by Ray Moller unless otherwise credited.

Acknowledgements:
Amsterdam, Van Gogh Museum,Vincent Van Gogh Museum Foundation : 15. Burstein Collection/
Corbis: 25. © Ralph Goings, All Rights Reserved 2004 tbc.Seavest Collection of Contemporary
American Realism: 9. © James P. Hawkins: 24bl. Kunsthistorisches Museum, Vienna/AKG
Images/Erich Lessing: 11. Kunstmuseum, Basel/Bridgeman Art Library: 21. Louvre, Paris/Bridgeman Art
Library: 19. Musée de l'Orangerie, Paris/Dagli Orti/The Art Archive: front cover main image, 16t, 17.
Musée des Beaux-Arts de Strasbourg-Photo A. Plisson: 7. Museo Civico ala Ponzone, Cremona/AKG
Images/Erich Lessing: 13. © 2003, Digital Image/Museum of Modern Art, New York.© photo Scala
Florence. © Claes Oldenburg and Coosje van Bruggen, All Rights Reserved 2004 tbc: 27. Presented by
Mrs H.K.Morton through the Contemporary Art Society 1969. The Tate, London. © Patrick Caulfield.
All rights reserved, © DACS London 2004: 23.

Every attempt has been made to clear copyright. Should there be any
inadvertent omission please apply to the publisher for rectification.

A CIP catalogue record for this book is available from the British Library

ISBN 978 0 7496 7358 1

Printed in China

Franklin Watts is a division of Hachette Children's Books.

Contents

What is a still life?

A still life is a picture of everyday **objects**. These are usually carefully chosen and placed in an **arrangement**.

▶ ▼ Fruit and flowers
Many artists are inspired by the colours and **textures** of fruit and flowers.

◀ Strange shapes
Other artists enjoy painting things with unusual shapes, such as musical instruments.

The artist chose these objects to make you think of your five **senses**.

▲ *The Five Senses*, Jacques Linard, 1638

What things could you taste in this picture?
What could you smell? What would feel
soft or hard? What could you look into?
What might you hear?

What to paint?

The objects in a still life usually have something in common. You could choose . . .

. . . things that are the same shape. Balls are round. ▶

◀ . . . things that go together. This lunchbox is packed with tasty food and drink.

Draw a still life
Draw a group of objects with something in common. This picture shows things from the seaside.

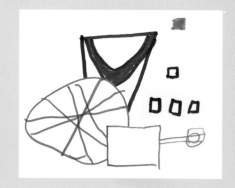

Can you see where light is shining
on the objects in the picture?

▲ *Relish*, Ralph Goings, 1994

This painting shows things that the artist
found on a table at an American café.
Spot a ketchup bottle, a napkin holder,
salt and pepper shakers, packets of sugar,
and a jar of relish.

Painting flowers

Artists can make flowers look very lifelike, or they may focus on their colours or shape.

▶ Pretty petals

Look at the petals of these flowers. Do they look lifelike to you?

▶ Daisy display

These flowers were painted with blobs of bright paint. They do not have much **detail**.

Flower focus
Draw a flower in a vase. Notice the shape of its petals and leaves. Are they round or pointy? Long or short?

▲ *A Bouquet of Flowers,*
Rachel Ruysch, about 1706

The detail in this painting makes the flowers
look very lifelike. But in real life, the artist
never saw all of these flowers together, because
they grow at different times of the year.

Painting food

Some artists like painting pictures of food.

Painting peas ▶
Artists may paint food in a dish, like these peas.

A careful arrangement
Sometimes, painters group vegetables and fruit in an interesting way, like this. ▼

Fruit and veg
Paint a picture of your favourite fruit and vegetables. Choose different shapes and colours.

Turn the picture upside-down.

🔺 *Market-Gardener or Joke With Vegetables,* Giuseppe Arcimboldo, 1590

You may think this picture just shows a bowl of vegetables. What can you see when you turn the book upside-down?

Line and shape

Before artists paint a still life, they often draw a **sketch** in pencil or ink.

Follow these steps to draw a picture of a mug.

The outline
1 Draw an outline of the mug. The outline shows its shape.

Shadows
2 See where light hits the mug. Where there is little or no light, add lines to show **shadows**.

More shadows
3 Where there is no light at all, add more lines to make the shadows darker.

▲ *Still Life with Coffee Pot,*
Vincent Van Gogh, 1888

Vincent Van Gogh often
drew sketches like this in letters
to his brother. He liked to paint
everyday things, as well as
the places he visited.

Lots of colours

Colours can make you feel a certain way about a painting.

▲ ▶ **Warm colours**
Red, orange and yellow are called warm colours. They make us think of sunshine, fire and the earth.

▲ ▶ **Cool colours**
Blue, green and grey are called cool colours. They remind us of water, sky and shade.

Which apples look ripe and ready to eat?
Which ones might be sharp and sour?

▲ *Apples and Biscuits,*
Paul Cézanne, about 1880

See how many colours Cézanne used to paint
these apples. There are many shades of red,
orange and yellow - and green, too.

Light

Artists use different shades of colour to show light and shadow. These help you to sense how things look and feel.

◀ Reflections

The pale patches on these balloons are **reflections**. This is where light is shining on the balloons.

▲ Painting reflections

Artists paint reflections either in a lighter colour than the rest of the object, or in white.

Looking at light

In a dark room, shine a torch on an object. Where does the light hit it? Can you see any reflections?

If you could touch these things, how would they feel?

▲ *Still Life With Figs,* Luis Meléndez, 1746

The light and shadows on these objects help show you which of them are rough, smooth or soft. Can you tell where the light is shining from?

Shapes and patterns

Sometimes artists are really interested in the shapes of objects.

▲ **All square**
A computer artist has changed this photo of a drum into a picture of hundreds of tiny squares. ▶

Showing shapes
Paint a still life in shapes and patterns. Choose something with a strong shape, such as this kite.

What objects can you see
in this picture?

▲ *Guitar and Clarinet*, Juan Gris, 1920

In this still life, Gris has used the same shapes
and lines over and over again. Can you spot
the lines and shapes that are repeated?

Viewpoints

Your viewpoint is where you are when you are looking at an object. You can see an object from above, from below or from the side.

▲ From above
From this angle, you can look into a mug.

▲ Side view
Seen from the side, a mug looks flat.

In front or behind? ▶
Objects in the front of a picture often hide part of the ones behind.

Choosing a viewpoint
Arrange objects for a still life. Choose a viewpoint to paint from. This picture is painted from above.

▲ *Pottery,* Patrick Caulfield, 1969

These vases, jugs, plates and bowls are shown from above and below, as well as from the side. The clear outlines and bright colours make each thing easy to see.

Arty tricks

Artists can make objects look very lifelike, like the ones on these pages.

▼Computer creation

This picture was created on a computer. Different photos of real things were put together to make this new image.

Try a trick
Draw a door with objects hanging on pegs. Add shadows to make them stand out.

Does it look as if you could touch the things in this picture?

◀ **Old Models, W. M. Harnett, 1892**

It's hard to believe that this is a flat picture. It is painted in great detail. The shadows make the objects seem to stick out, as if they were real.

Still life sculptures

Some modern artists make still life **sculptures**.

▼ **Sandal sculpture**
You can see sculptures from the front, back and sides. This sculpture is made of clay.

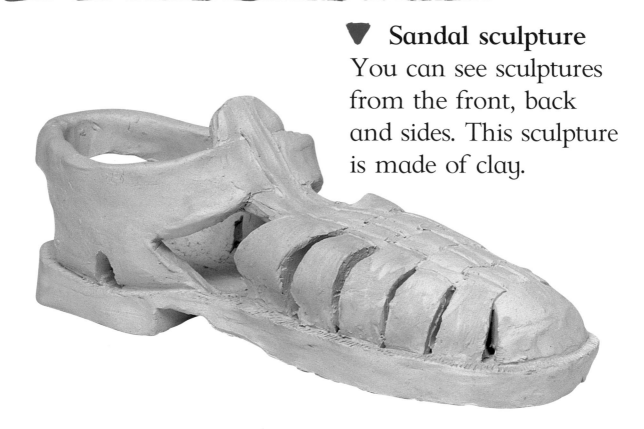

Make a still life sculpture
Use modelling clay to make a still life sculpture. Look around your home for everyday objects to copy.

Imagine eating a slice of cake that is as tall as a person and as long as a car!

▲ *Floor Cake,* **Claes Oldenburg, 1962**

Oldenburg made this huge slice of cake from strong fabric and stuffed it with foam. He has also used fabric to make an enormous burger, and giant furry ice lollies.

Quiz

1. What do these still life objects have in common?

2. Find the still life pictures in the book that show flowers. Find the pictures with food.

3. Which of these are warm colours? Which are cool colours? Find more warm and cool colours in the book.

4. Where is light shining on this balloon? Look at the pictures in the book to find more reflections.

5. Which shapes can you see in this still life picture?

square   circle   triangle

Glossary

arrangement   How objects are placed in a group. A still life is an arrangement of objects.

detail   A small part of a picture that you can see when you look carefully. Details often make pictures look more lifelike.

object   A thing that is not alive, but can be seen or touched. A still life is a picture of objects.

reflection   An area of a painting where light shines against an object.

sculpture   Artwork that can be seen from all sides.

senses   People have five senses. These are seeing, hearing, touching, smelling and tasting.

shadow   A dark area of a painting where light does not shine.

sketch   A rough drawing showing an idea or arrangement. Artists often do sketches for a painting.

texture   How things feel - for example, smooth or rough.

Websites

www.sanford-artedventures.com
Lots of art ideas for children to try, including a step-by-step Fruity Still Life.

www.artcyclopedia.com
Enter 'still life' in the search box to see lots of still life pictures, or enter the name of an artist.

http://www.ibiblio.org/wm/paint
The artists' index includes information on van Gogh, Cezanne and Gris.

www.artlex.com
Enter 'still life' in this online art dictionary to find many pictures of still lifes, divided into four historical periods.

Note to parents and teachers
Every effort has been made by the Publishers to ensure that these websites are suitable for children. However, because of the nature of the Internet, it is impossible to guarantee that the contents of these sites will not be altered. We strongly advise that Internet access is supervised by a responsible adult.

Index